The Golden Years of British
TRAMS

Colin Garratt
on the work of
Henry Priestly
In association with The National Tramway Museum

Bounty Books

The National Tramway Museum

In the beginning there was no time and no place. Just men with a mission and a desperate desire to rescue, store and restore as many trams as possible during the "Termination Terror" of the 1950s.

By stealth or with a fanfare, trams are coming back on track – but those at the National Tramway Museum are the originals!

This award winning "Museum on the Move" has gradually been developed to become one of the finest transport museums in the country, and if you haven't visited for several years you must! It's a continually changing and ever-fascinating place.

The National Tramway Museum, Crich, Derbyshire
Tel: 01773 854321

First published in 1995 by Milepost Publishing
in conjunction with Arcturus Publishing Ltd,
for Bookmart Ltd.

Milepost Publishing is a division of Milepost 92 ½
Newton Harcourt,
Leicestershire LE8 9FH
Tel: 0116 2593001

Milepost 92 ½ is Colin Garratt's Audio Visual Production,
Presentation and Photographic Service for the Railway Industry.

This edition published in 2007 by Bounty Books,
a division of Octopus Publishing Group Ltd
2–4 Heron Quays, London E14 4JP

An Hachette Livre UK Company

ISBN: 978-0-753714-50-8

A CIP catalogue record for this book is available from the British Library

Printed and bound in China

INTRODUCTION

Henry Priestley's tramway photographs represent the finest visual legacy of that age in existence. Most of his negatives are in the archives of the National Tramway Museum at Crich in Derbyshire and it was there that myself along with Glynn Wilton, the curator, conceived the idea of bringing together some of the best of Henry Priestley's work in one superb book which would not only record, but also evoke the tramway era in Britain. Henry Priestley was born at South Ossett in the West Riding during the reign of King Edward VII. He taught chemistry and physics before gaining an MA from London University. He was headmaster of Brunts Grammar School, Mansfield from 1950 until 1975.

Excursions to photograph tramways were often on his Sunbeam Lion 600cc motor cycle which appears in several pictures. In later years he used a 1933 Wolseley, which also appears as a strategic part of many compositions. Henry Priestley married in 1938 and the magnificent picture which adorns the rear of the jacket was taken on his honeymoon.

Henry Priestley along with his wife Margaret continue to enjoy a full and active life and the task of producing this book has been made infinitely more enjoyable by his willingness and enthusiasm to contribute his amazing technical knowledge and store of memories. He recalls with vigour and clarity the taking of each picture notwithstanding that many were done over half a century ago.

Henry Priestley recalls vivid experiences with tramways from as early as the age of four and, after taking up photography in the 1920's, has always put great thought and care into his pictures. Most shots are hand held; he felt tripods of the time unsteady and often held his camera against a tramcar bulkhead, on a step or a windowsill. He strove to place the tram into its wider social context and herein lies part of the magic of his work, but he exercised an equal fascination for the delicate tapestries of overhead wiring and installations along with the texture and pattern of tram tracks and road surfaces. He liked to look down on track layouts with angles from balconies and flats, top decks of trams and railway bridges. Failing these, he would open the sunshine roof of his Wolseley and stand up on the seat. "Trackwork is much better seen from slightly above, especially if you've a slanting shadow; ideally you need to be at right angles to the sun," says Henry Priestley. And he recorded details meticulously, checking locations on a street map.

Always the tram is shown fully in its setting. He gives us countless details to help recreate this vanished world of the thirties, forties and fifties. A world of corner shops, terraced houses, horses and handcarts, of unrestricted cigarette advertising. Few motorcars, and those mostly coloured black. Schoolboys in short trousers. A world where people could cross the road diagonally and even pause for a chat without fear of traffic, and a child in a pushchair could be left safely outside a shop. Only in the later pictures are there signs of change; motorcyclists with helmets begin to appear, and there are painted road markings, standardised road signs and even a few television aerials, H or X shaped.

The absence of these things adds fascination to the earlier shots, and makes us realise for all we have gained we have lost a great deal. For the removal of tram tracks was part of a process of dismemberment of the closely-knit social, commercial and structural fabric of British cities so much of which took place between the 1930's and 1970's. Once the nation's tramways had been decimated – the last system being Glasgow in 1962 – the iniquitous Beeching Act commenced the same decimation of our railway network, so tearing the heart out of the fabric of society and co-ordinated community life. We have paid dearly for the loss of our trams and railways and we look upon our national leaders to ensure their return. Germany, despite the scale of its post-war reconstruction, kept people working and living in cities in sufficient numbers to sustain shops and local amenities, and held on to and developed the tramway networks which bound the whole fabric together. Britain is now having to rediscover the tramway, the terraced house and the corner shop at far greater cost than would have been the case if these had all been allowed to remain and develop naturally.

Much is now written about "traffic calming"; these words contain an indictment of those who allowed traffic to reach proportions where it needed calming. Henry Priestley's pictures show us highways functioning as means of access, but so often these have been turned into barriers of solid traffic, just one of the ways in which uncontrolled motor car use has distorted life.

Mistaken accounting policies for tramways made no provision for renewals and rendered them vulnerable to replacement by buses from the late 1920's onwards. Ironically, the buses which replaced trams have proved less effective than rail vehicles at providing a form of transport acceptable to motorists as an alternative to their cars. So strategies to combat traffic growth have led to a new generation of trams; these, and the pictures in this book clearly indicate that we would have been far better off had our basic tramway infrastructure been maintained and developed.

Finally, I extend my warmest thanks to Glynn Wilton for his friendship and skill in producing the finest prints possible along with his help in the book's design. No less to Ian Yearsley who has contributed so much to the captions from his incomparable tramway knowledge, his understanding of social history and his unfailing sense of humour which bursts through the captions like rays of vibrant sunlight.

I would also like to thank Winstan Bond and Rosy Thacker of the National Tramway Museum for their support and to add that anyone inspired by the contents of this book should visit the National Tramway Museum in Crich. With over 50 fully restored trams – most in full working order – this working museum constitutes one of the finest days out in Britain providing guaranteed fascination for both sexes of all ages.

Colin Garratt,
Milepost 92 $^{1}/_{2}$,
Newton Harcourt,
Leicestershire,
England.

TRAMS
OF NORTHERN BRITAIN

MILEPOST

INTRODUCTION

The light, the landscapes and the industries provide the Northern settings for Henry Priestley's tramway photographs. Canaletto would have refused to paint in the Northern mists, but this is Laurence Lowry country. The grime of industry and a myriad domestic coal fires darkened the buildings; apart from a few signs and advertisements, the tram was often the only splash of colour in an urban scene.

Henry Priestley travelled widely to record tramway images. One week in 1954 found him on successive days in Glasgow, Aberdeen, Edinburgh and Liverpool. And what a variety to see! Tramway reserved sleeper tracks to new estates formed part of urban planning in Liverpool and Leeds; by contrast, trams and tracks were squeezed into narrow streets in Dundee.

It was a world less sophisticated than today, where a tram ride to the park was an afternoon out, and most shops were locally owned. Only in a few late shots do self-service appear, and the hypermarket is as far away in the future as the personal computer.

Henry Priestley records these vistas on a wide screen, and if you are tempted to step into them and explore, why not? The Past may be a far country, but always worth a visit.

Dublin was different. The front balcony of a Dublin United car gives a view from Dalkey Depot of the Irish standard 5ft 3in gauge track, even more impressive in the street than on the main line railways. And how that wall on the right must have thrown back the echoes as the car ahead pulled away!

Previous spread
To save the cost of renewing tram tracks, many towns in the 1930's changed to trolleybuses. On 25 June 1938 Henry Priestley parked his motorbike JP 364 at Dod-Lea to record 18- year old Huddersfield balcony car 120. Already the extra wires are in place for trolleybuses, and the conductor has his bamboo pole hooked over the trolley pole, ready to turn it for the journey back to town.

City centres in the 1950's, smoky grey and granite, before the motor car took over.
Top left in Leeds contrasts a 1930-built ex-London car with a 1926 Leeds design; *Below left and top right* are examples of Leeds 1931 Horsfield styling, while *below right* is one of Aberdeen's 1949 centre entrance cars.

The sheer emptiness of roads, still possible in Leeds, *above left,* where blue liveried Horsfield car 160 sails past railway posters in Marsh Lane in May, 1939, possible too in August that year in Gateshead, *below left,* where children cross unworried by single deck front exit car 16 as it emerges from Sunderland Road depot. And still to be found in Sheffield in 1952, *above*, where 1935-built standard car 226's cream and blue paintwork glistens among the grime of the steelworks. The long shelters house queues of workers at shift-change times; a line of six trams could move 500 people.

Over page
Another photographer might have moved the wheelbarrow and tidied the clutter, or chosen another angle to record this depot interior in Halifax. But Henry Priestley gives it all, the basic maintenance facilities that ensured that these sturdy and comfortable 3ft 6in gauge cars climbed safely up and down in a town with scarcely more than a few yards of level track. This is one of the earliest shots in this book, taken two days before Christmas, 1936.

View from a tram top as ex-London Feltham 534 and a 1920's Chamberlain car approach with Leeds Parish Church as a backdrop.

Two of Glasgow's much-rebuilt standard cars in George Square, in 1954, car 186 dates from 1913, rebuilt in 1930.

Dundee, like Glasgow and Leeds, changed from trolley pole to bow collector. Car 38, seen in 1955, dates from 1921.

Liverpool used trolley poles to the end. 1937-built car 938 passes Coronation decorations in Parker Street, June 1953.

Many-textured road surfaces, uncluttered by motor traffic. 1932-style Edinburgh car 180 reverses at Merchiston siding, *left*, watched by a crew with summer white tops to their hats in July 1955. *Above*, Two Leeds Chamberlain design cars of 1926/27 in full pre-war blue livery at Balm Road terminus in May 1939. Cigarettes advertised freely and Alexander's Ragtime Band at the Strand Cinema.

Rain and poor light call forth the photographer's skill. Two views of Sunderland on 30 October 1953 show, *below left*, a much rebuilt 1903 car, no. 63 at Derwent Street, little more than a dark reflection on the glistening setts, and, *above*, car 24 at Fulwell on smooth tarmacadam paved track. This car was built in 1933 using the body of a Mansfield tram; in all Sunderland collected second-hand bargains from eight towns. In Sheffield, *top left*, 1921-built car 382 turns right at Hunter's Bar while an RAC motorcycle patrolman waits for passengers to board car 247, beyond.

Whether following the road or cutting across country, reserved tracks gave trams a chance to show their speed and cost less to build than paved street tracks. These examples in Leeds are at Roundhay Park, *top* and *below, left*, and in Middleton Woods, above. The Middleton light railway left the roads completely to provide a direct route to a large housing estate. Leeds Horsfield tramcars are at home in these surroundings, yet what a contrast with city streets!

Smoke still pours out of a works chimney in aptly named Vulcan Road, Sheffield, on Palm Sunday, 1958, while another photographer records the tram used by Henry Priestley to capture the scene, *left*, now deserted, but thronged at every shift change. *Above* the water tower of Walton prison forms a grim backdrop in February 1955 to 1937-built Liverpool streamline car 166.

The broad view at Cabin station in August 1958, where Blackpool's tramroad to Fleetwood, *top left*, displays tramcars dating from 1928 to 1953; a similar view of Blackpool's promenade at Foxhall out of season in April 1953, *bottom left*, shows English Electric railcoaches of 1934 in two paint-styles. English Electric also built Bradford car 257 in 1919, seen with others, *centre left*, outside Thornbury Depot in July 1939. Suburban and city settings *this page* for Sheffield tramcars 222 of 1935 at Handsworth in 1930 and 126 of 1923 using the trolley reverser at Suffolk Street in 1952. Will the man in a motorised invalid carriage catch up with the tram?

Trams in light traffic at Shore Road, Belfast with former horse tram 244 doing snowplough duty in 1951, *top*; Car 132 of 1910, now preserved, passes Cottingham Road, Hull in 1938, *above*; Forster Square, Bradford with car 241 in 1938, *top right*; and Marsh Lane/York Street junction, Leeds with blue liveried 1931 Horsfield car 239 in May 1939.

Like Bradford, Blackburn used four foot gauge track. Its cars were solid, foursquare in dark green and ivory. *Left*, car 65, a 1920's rebuild of a 1900 Milnes product, stands among Blackburn and Ribble buses at the Railway Station in April 1939. Much rebuilt also is Newcastle car 29 at Gateshead station in August 1939 *top right*; and *below right* Liverpool 944, built only the previous year, shows off the pre-war olive green livery at Lodge Lane junction in May 1938.

Previous spread
Camera held firmly against the bulkhead door, Henry Priestley captures Sheffield 1933-built car 132, still in the old dark blue livery, as it heads from Abbey Lane towards the city across the junction with the Meadowhead route. The driver has stood aside to reveal his controller, left, and the hand brake handle and track brake wheel, right.

A tram under a bridge is an actor on a stage. Oldfield Lane bridge sets the scene for blue-liveried Leeds Horsfield 204 in March 1938, *top left*; while red-painted car 167 passes a parade of pre-war petrol pumps near Burley Road bridge in April 1954 *below*. In the same year in Liverpool, Walton station bridge, *above*, carries a co-op advert with strong echoes of 1951 Festival of Britain styling; the tram underneath dates from 1937.

Horse-drawn vehicles figure strongly here, a Clydesdale heavy horse pulls a lurry past ex-Manchester car 48 of 1930-32 at Queen's Cross depot junction, Aberdeen in 1954 *top left*, while *below left* a rag and bone man leads his pony off the tram tracks as Manchester 1927-built car 1009 loads passengers at Hulme Church in August 1938, a scene now dominated by the Chester Road flyover, whilst *above*, a Shire heavy draught horse pulls a heavy cart full of builder's material at the Park Avenue/Laisteridge Lane junction in Bradford. The tram dates from 1920, the date is Saturday 2 July 1938, and Bradford City's football ground is just down the road.

Take the tram to the corner shop, for aniseed cough balsam at Compton Road terminus Leeds, *bottom left*, where Chamberlain car 443 in March 1938 has yet to exchange its trolleypole for a bow collector, or for White Rose Oil or an Echo radio at Tottington terminus, Bury, *top left*, in April 1937, where 1926-built car 57 has just arrived. Or visit the pawnbrokers and outfitters on Wakefield Road, Bradford, *above*, where car 31 takes power from the positive trolleybus wire as it climbs the hill.

The tram indoors, in depots and repair workshops, in 1937 at Dundee's Lochee depot *top left*, in 1936 at Stockport Mersey Square *top right*, in 1938 at Bradford's Thornbury depot *bottom left*, and in 1954 in Kirkstall Road works, Leeds, *bottom right*. The Bradford line-up is not quite what it seems; all these cars have been given new numbers to avoid awkward questions about a batch of cars with poor bodywork which had to be scrapped early.

Crowds spilling off the pavements, in St Nicholas Street, Aberdeen, *left*, where olive green painted car 105, rugged and sturdy, swings from single track into a passing loop in August 1955. At Blackburn in April 1939, *top right*, Milnes bogie car 62 heads for Preston New Road past Woolworth's 3d and 6d Stores at Salford junctions, and wide-bodied Lochee car 24 takes the centre track in Dundee High Street in August 1955, *bottom right*.

Trams and urchins in Liverpool: Both pictures were taken on 16 October 1954, with 1937-built streamline car 962 at Everton road junction, *left*, and sister-car 963 at the corner of Eastbourne Street and Fitzclarence Street. How those large cars swept around the sinuous curves between the soot-grimed buildings! Overhead wiring above 963 has already been prepared for the change to bow collectors which never took place in Liverpool.

Over page
The lower end of the Middleton reserved track light railway in Leeds ran through industrial wasteland landscapes. Children carry jars indicating a visit to Parkside newt ponds nearby. Car 257, in the distance, is one of those built specially for this route in 1935.

Child's eye view of trams. In Leeds, *top left*, car 151 still with a trolleypole in March 1938, pauses at the Barley Mow loop, Bramley. In Manchester, car 357 is about to turn from Princess Road into Denmark Road in August 1938, *bottom left*, car 1017 is followed by a heavily-laden lorry out of Booth Street West, *this page, top*, and people cross casually behind car 876 at Miles Platting, *this page, bottom*, while Heginbottom's tripe works' van pushes ahead.

Two streets, both with tramtracks: *Above*, Car 1024 was built by Liverpool in 1936 and came to Glasgow in February 1954; two months later Henry Priestley saw it at St George's Cross. The Yorkshire Penny Bank marks the corner at Kirkgate, Leeds, in May 1939, *top right*, and by this time all Leeds cars, like 125 here, carry bow collectors. By 1954, television aerials have begun to sprout at Abbey Hill, Edinburgh, *bottom right*, where the traffic policeman has just waved 1936-built car 45 on its way, though his duties do not seem otherwise too demanding.

Trams on the Irish broad gauge: Dublin United Tramways built car 287 in 1927, and, *above*, it pauses outside Harcourt Street Station in April 1939. Even after Dublin's last tram ran in 1949, the Great Northern Railway (Ireland) continued to run its Hill of Howth tramway; in August 1956, *right*, car 6 of the original 1900 batch waits at Howth Station for the run to Sutton. Track is laid GNR(I) fashion with bullhead rail, keyed inside so that one platelayer can check both rails at once.

The textured road surface of setts and tram rails fascinated Henry Priestley at Liverpool, *above*, where car 948 prepares to round the curve at Aubrey Street in October 1954, and in Leeds at Balm Road Mills in May 1939, *top right*, where the single track section shows an obvious candidate for road widening. The factory chimney overshadows the line of washing behind the houses. Rain in Sunderland in October 1953 gives reflections of car 24, rebuilt in 1933 from a Mansfield tramcar, *bottom right*. The track to the right leads to the football ground.

Classic Henry Priestley planning for this top deck view of Leeds 176 at Rookwood, *above*, taken in August 1959. Careful composition too at Sea Beach, Aberdeen, *top right*, where the long queue barriers speak of summer crowds, though only a few will board post-war centre entrance car 39 on this August day in 1955. Tramway extension and new estates went together in Leeds, *bottom right*, with ex-London car 549 at Middleton Ring Road.

The date is 2 August 1938 and the photographer's motor-car is legally parked alongside the sign forbidding waiting on odd dates in Brook Street, Manchester, *top left*, as 1928-built car 352 approaches the Grosvenor Street junction. The same motor-car appears, *above*, at Westhoughton terminus in April 1938, where Bolton tramcar 99, much rebuilt from a 1910 model, boldly displays route letter E. Somewhat grander limousines park in Dublin's O'Connell Street, *bottom left*, in April 1939 while balcony car 289 reverses at Nelson Pillar.

Trams framed by bridges: At Leith Trinity Road, Edinburgh car 304 of 1923 follows an S-shaped course to negotiate the corner in April 1954, *top left*, while 1935 Edinburgh standard car 164 rumbles across Bernard Street swing bridge, *bottom left*. Gateshead car 29, seen in August 1939 beneath Gateshead Station arch, *above*, is a rebuild of an 1899 Liverpool car. The crossover on interlaced track would have caught Henry Priestley's eye.

Over Page
Child's eye view of a holiday town with 1938 fashions, a speeding cyclist, visitors' cars parked, and two tramcars picking up and setting down passengers. The scene is Church Street, Blackpool; balcony cars 146 and 160 date from 1924 and 1927. The Yorkshire Penny Bank has a branch in this Lancashire resort.

City streets, incomplete without tracks and wires. Newcastle's Grainger Street in August 1937 already has a crossing of trolleybus wires, *above*, front-exit tramcar 291 is a standard vehicle of 1921-1926 build. Bradford Forster Square, *top right*, already has some trolleybus wiring in July 1939, car 255 was built as recently as 1930. With Leeds parish church as background in May 1951, *bottom right*, Chamberlain car 131 shows the later blue livery.

One tramcar, two motor-cars, one pedestrian, a motor-cycle combination and a tradesmen's delivery cyclist share Liverpool's Walton Lane on a misty day in April 1954, *top left*, while works car 2 and Lochee car 19 pass in North Tay Street, Dundee in August 1955, *bottom left*. Also in 1955, *above*, Horsfield cars 237 and 247 of 1931/2 reverse at Meanwood Terminus, Leeds, in June sunshine.

These three Edinburgh flat roof standard cars, seen at Goldenacre, *above*, in April 1954, date from 1933 and 1927. In Sheffield, *top right*, car 258 of 1937 waits for car 65 of 1930 to clear the single track at Malin Bridge in June 1938. Some tracks are already tarred over at Brownlow Hill junction, *bottom right*, in May 1955, where Liverpool tramcars 909 and 914, both dating from 1936, look well in post-war livery. Already the international standard No Entry signs have appeared.

The two Bradford trams, *top left*, at the Alhambra in July 1939, are low-height cars for the Greengates route. In the background, right is a single deck trolleybus, on left a two-wheeled horse-drawn cart. *Bottom left*, the slanting sunshine at Swinegate depot entrance, Leeds, picks out details of the track as car 74, now in red livery, heads for Belle Isle. Trackwork details at Govan, Glasgow, show up well as standard car 365, 1930 rebuild of a 1905 vehicle, crosses the junction, *above*.

Suburban sleeper tracks and traffic islands, in Liverpool, *top left*, at Black Horse loop, and at Broad Green Hospital, *top right*, both with 1937-built cars in April 1954; and in the same month at Anniesland, Glasgow, *bottom left*, with standard hex-dash car 154 of 1913. In August 1938, *bottom right*, Salford 348, formerly a front-exit car, is at Irlams o'th' Height terminus.

Tram follows traffic at Garston, Liverpool in April 1952, *above*, while traffic waits for tram to turn left at Upper Brook Street, Manchester in August 1938, *below*. In the far distance, parked beyond the crossing, is the photographer's car.

A passenger alights in the roadway from Liverpool car 986 at Crown Street in April 1954, *above*, and in the same month ex-Liverpool car 1018 approaches St George's Cross, Glasgow, *below*. Massey's on the left already offers self-service, but still does deliveries by bicycle with basket.

Sheffield briefly tried a colour scheme of two shades of green, carried by car 253 on a grey day at Pitsmoor in July 1952, *top left*. The schoolboy, right, has found something far more fascinating! The city quickly returned to the blue and cream colours carried by car 234 at Holme Lane in September 1951, *bottom left*. The quality of Sheffield's asphalt paving shows up, even around depot approach tracks. Another depot approach, *above*, this time sett-paved, is at Queens Road where in October 1957 a zebra crossing has appeared, though tramcar, police box, shelter and street furniture reflect early Sheffield patterns.

Over Page
Sunlight filters down into Langside Depot, Glasgow, in August 1955. Cleaners' galleries, suspended from the roof, dominate the scene. A difficult exposure, so Henry Priestley holds the camera against the bulkhead of standard car 122 to record its controls as well as the standard car, Coronation and works car in one almost cloister-like scene.

Track repairs, at Highfields, Sheffield, in May 1952, *top left*; Edge Lane, Liverpool, in April 1954, *bottom left*; and The Gynn, Blackpool, in April 1952, *above*. This is pick and shovel work, only one pneumatic drill in sight. No traffic cones, safety helmets, or high visibility clothing. Sheffield and Liverpool scenes show why reserved sleeper track was always cheaper to build and maintain; there was no road surface to lift before getting at the track

Henry Priestley tried to record textures of road surfaces, buildings, ironwork, along with the trams and the track. In Dundee, *above*, in August 1955 Lochee car 24 approaches track worn below the level of the setts. Outside Anfield Cemetery, Liverpool, *top right*, points are cleaned in April 1954 with no more than a red flag to warn oncoming traffic on the heavily patched road surface. In the same month, *bottom right*, Castle Junction, Aberdeen offers an uncompromising pattern of setts, tracks and granite buildings, with 1949-built car 22 among the sturdy products of the 1920's.

Hull 148 is the centre of an animated street scene in June 1938 at Dairycoates, *top left*, Dundee car 5, dating back to 1900, approaches the West Port/North Tay Street junction in August 1955, *bottom left*, and in the same month two Aberdeen cars pass on one of the St Nicholas Street loops (compare with earlier view), *above*.

Looking down on four foot gauge tracks, from one Bradford balcony to another, car 23 of 1929 on Wibsey Hill at Thornton Lane, *above*, in July 1938, and at Blackburn car 45, rebuilt in the 1920's from 1900 open top, *below*, as it approaches the Darwen boundary in April 1939. The factory chimney showing above the field gives an almost surrealist atmosphere to the scene.

TRAMS
OF SOUTHERN BRITAIN

MILEPOST 92½

INTRODUCTION

Some of Henry Priestley's journeys south to photograph trams were only just in time, for tramways were abandoned early in many places. So he recorded the tramways of Bath, Bristol, Merthyr, Reading and Coventry, all of which ceased running before or early in the second world war.

This section also includes some of his London and Birmingham pictures, and a tribute to the many vistas offered by the Llandudno & Colwyn Bay line. London with the complexity of its conduit trackwork provided many subjects for his camera, both north of the Thames and south, while Birmingham pre-war offered contrasts between the city's own main roads and the tortuous routes it took over from the Birmingham & Midland company.

Was it the weather that led to so many smaller towns in the south to use open top tramcars? Did the absence of heavy industry give a clarity to the atmosphere, as well as leaving buildings less covered in grime than in the northern cities? Whatever it was, Henry Priestley used the same techniques of photography, looking for a high vantage point, sun shining across the tracks, movement and animation in the street scenes, and always plenty of detail.

Here too, you feel you can almost step into the picture. And why not?

Everything about this scene speaks of elegance, whether the mid-1890s styling of Bristol Tramways and Carriage Company car 123, built by Milnes in 1900, or the celebratory scrollwork adorning the tram stop sign, or the April 1939 fashions of the ladies alighting from the tramcar in Ashton Road. Fashion drawings at this period depicted ladies of unbelievable slimness, but the diet of the time tended less towards weight than that of today, and the average height of people was slightly less. The Belisha beacon speaks of growing motor traffic, though the road is still relatively empty, and metal studs rather than zebra stripes mark the crossing on the road surface.

Previous spread

So much of the tramway story is caught up in this London Transport car, recorded by Henry Priestley on the corner of Camden Road and Caledonian Road in July 1938. Built by Brush in 1909 as Metropolitan Electric Tramways class H car 238, it has been updated in various ways before becoming London Transport car 2170 in 1933. It is running on the centre slot conduit current collection system of the former London County Council lines, but already the overhead wires are in place for trolleybuses that will replace tram route 59 in October. Throughout 1938 there were fears of war, leading to the Munich meetings in September, and already in July the sign on the Tufnell Park Garage appeals for volunteers for the Air Raid Precautions service. Meanwhile the limousine with gleaming hinges to its folding top forges ahead; the tramcar will turn left, crossing behind it.

Core of the vast London tramway network was the former London County Council system, much of which had centre-slot conduit current collection instead of conventional overhead wires. Cars of class E3, built in 1930-31 with metal bodywork to run through the Kingsway Subway, are seen on route 31, *top left*, from Hackney to Battersea and Wandsworth in July 1938, while *above*, ex-Metropolitan Electric car 2196 pauses for traffic lights alongside Dorothy's guaranteed Perms on Seven Sisters Road near Finsbury Park Station. Overhead wires in both pictures are for the new trolleybuses. South of the Thames, HR2 class car 1887 modernised in the 1930s along with many E1 class cars, swings through the Blackheath Hill loop on Lewisham Road, *bottom left*, in September 1951.

Llandudno & Colwyn Bay Electric, with all its timeless elegance. Have the couple just alighted from ex-Bournemouth car 15 at Benarth Road, *top left*, to look at a prospective home for their retirement? Will they consider the trams, the lattice pole and the shelter made out of old tramcar bulkhead doors, as assets to the neighbourhood? Some of those doors came from cars like number 17, seen entering private right of way, *bottom left*, on the Little Orme. Both these were taken in August 1954; in September 1953 car 15 at Maesgwyn, *right*, leaves the section of single track made necessary when the sea eroded the track on the right. This was a private toll road belonging to the tramway company.

Over page
Plymouth built its last new cars in 1926-27, and this car, 166 seen at Peverell in August 1938, was the last of the batch. Originally on bogies, most, like this one, were later mounted on a four wheeled truck. Its styling, advanced in the mid-1920's, was quickly overtaken by the jazzy styles epitomised by the lady on the left. And also by the new double deck buses.

Not all London's streets are wide, and other traffic has to squeeze past the trams. On Camden Road approaching the High Street, ex-Walthamstow 1927-built car 2048, together with E1 1156 and two buses, *above*, pose a problem for the learner driver in the sports car in June 1938. Another close squeeze for E3 car 202, one of those built in 1931 for Leyton, *top right*, running on overhead wires at Leytonstone Church in July 1938; signal lights for the single track ahead are on the pole on the left. At Highbury, *bottom right*, E3 car 1949 in June 1938 passes a Luton-head van of the type originally designed to carry light but bulky loads of straw hats, while the Highbury Fish Restaurant offers generous helpings for ninepence.

White-gloved police constable directs traffic in Colwyn Bay in May 1953, *above*, including two Crosville buses and Llandudno car 2, still with its Accrington bogies. In Birmingham, *top right*, a white macintosh coat makes the policeman on duty readily visible at Saltley where the Washwood Heath and Alum Rock routes divide. 798 and 789 are Brush-built air-braked cars of 1928-29. Same distinctive uniform for a constable at the Summer Row, Birmingham, *bottom right*, as Smethwick-bound car 196 heads into Sand Pits Parade. The bow-collector equipped car behind is on route 32 and will turn into Newhall Hill.

So often in a tram depot there was a feeling of Marie Celeste mystery, of tasks left half-finished by unseen engineering staff. In Merthyr Tydfil's depot, *left*, built on the site of the Penydaren Ironworks, Henry Priestley lets us look in April 1938 through the windscreen of ex-Birmingham car 6 at ex-Birmingham & Midland car 15 and car 5, one of Merthyr's original single deck fleet of 1900, piled high with spare seats. In Birmingham, *above*, he takes us into the far corner of Hockley Depot in March 1939, only a few weeks before it ceased to house trams. The handcart's inscription BCT&O refers to Birmingham Corporation Tramways & Omnibuses. Balcony car 183 of 1906 became one of those stored as a strategic reserve fleet in wartime. Cars 589, 626 and 510 date from 1920-21 and continued in service on other routes.

Over page
How London's conduit system filled the street surfaces with tramway ironmongery! At York Road terminus, Wandsworth, in April 1948, the points have been set in both running rail and conduit for 1931-built E3 car 205. The trolleybus wiring here vanished at the same time as the Wandsworth route trams in 1950. Over the wall on the left is Young's brewery, and today this is known as Ram Street.

In June 1939 Graham Road, *top left*, shows London Transport in transition. 1907-built E1 car 881 is flanked by an open staircase bus and a bus of the latest STL variety. A trolleybus flashes past, and a 1920s taxi has just been hailed. In April 1939 in Birmingham, *bottom left*, car 102 picks up passengers on Dudley Road at Icknield Port Road while a mother attempts to cross the road with a pram. In August 1939 Cardiff car 31, *top right*, enters the single track at Hayes Bridge, and in the same month Bedworth-bound Coventry car 66, still only a few years old, approaches the Burges junction, *bottom right*.

It is August 1953, and Llandudno ex-Bournemouth car 14 has a good load of passengers at the Mostyn Street corner, *left*.
A well-loaded open top car always looked like a window-box full of flowers. Motor car registrations indicate that
Llandudno has visitors from Caernarvonshire, Manchester and London. And the Crosville bus on the left looks like an
early Leyland TD1, already over 20 years old. Looking in the other direction towards the West Shore terminus, *above*, a
boy tries out his bicycle across the tram tracks in front of ex-Accrington car 4.

Birmingham 634, built 1921 as a balcony car, slows for Short Heath terminus in April 1953, *top left*, where a modern No Entry sign is lit by a gas lamp. Years later, this was the site of a short-lived guided busway. At the Gravelly junction, *bottom left*, Birmingham 647, one of a 1923-24 batch by the Midland Railway Carriage & Wagon Company, heads towards the city in September 1937. Two months before final closure in 1953, car 543 heads through the back streets near Miller Street Depot, *top right*.

Over page
Car number 8 of the Merthyr Electric Traction & Lighting Company's fleet was built at the Birmingham & Midland Tramways' Tividale Works, sometime between 1913 and 1916. Merthyr bought it in 1929, and here Henry Priestley takes a child's eye view of it in Penydaren Road in April 1938.

A succession of railway bridges provide a stage-like setting for trams. Cardiff low-height car 100 vanishes beneath the former Taff Vale Railway bridge near Queen Street station, *top left*, in September 1937. Excursions advertised include one to Oxford, including lunch and a visit to the Morris car works, all for 12s 6d, or 62$^1/_2$p. Beneath the shadows of Wandsworth Town station bridge, London, *bottom left*, E3 car 203 of 1931 swings left on to double track to catch any motorist unawares in June 1949. Orthochromatic film not only records the red of the trams and trolleybuses as solid black, but also the amber top of the belisha beacon. Today this area is pedestrianised and gentrified. And *above*, back to Cardiff for the other side of the Taff Vale bridge with car 101, the prototype Brush low-height car of 1923. Henry Priestley had to get special permission to photograph from here; he is standing on the ex-Rhymney Railway bridge over Newport Road, this time in August 1939.

Leicester 144 at the Clock Tower in June 1937, *left*, with Stone's pointing the way forward with its television sign. Traffic jostles trams here, and also *above* in Coventry's Broadgate in August 1939, with cars 58, 50 and 53 bound for Stoke and Bell Green. Bomb damage the following year and subsequent rebuilding have changed Coventry's centre almost out of recognition.

Over page
An animated scene to delight the heart of Henry Priestley, at Park Street on the boundary between Grimsby and Cleethorpes, in April 1937, during the three months when Grimsby had converted its part of the through route to trolleybuses, but Cleethorpes had yet to do so. Car 57 originated with the Great Grimsby Street Tramways Company, which sold half its line to Grimsby in 1925 and the remaining two miles to Cleethorpes in 1936. New trolleybus poles are going up in the background, meanwhile the road is thronged with people changing from trolleybus to tram.

In postwar London suburbs the photographer could be an object of curiosity for small boys whose tailored jackets, coats and caps, along with short trousers and long socks, give a flavour of the period almost as much as the trams themselves do. Rebuilt 1910 E1 car 1396 is reversing at Battersea Bridge approach in April 1950, *above*; disconnected tracks curve into the riverside permanent way yard. At Greenwich Church, *top right*, another rebuilt E1, car 985 of 1907, has just arrived in April 1949. The Addington Street triangle, *bottom right*, was one of the last new pieces of conduit trackwork laid in London. Visible through the gap in the buildings in April 1950 are the platform canopies of Waterloo Station; a British Railways ex-LMS six-ton Scammell mechanical horse is parked on the left. The small boy in the Daniel Neal of Portman Square topcoat is far more interested in the newly-laid mass of steel in the street.

Parked cars and bicycles fill up the space between trams and the kerb in Leicester in May 1938, where *top left* cars 106 and 152 pass at the Great Central Street junction, and *bottom left* car 59 pursues a cyclist while number 76, now preserved at the National Tramway Museum, waits at traffic lights in Granby Street. Humberstone Gate, Leicester, *top right*, offers three tracks, three tramcars, an underground lavatory and a motorist about to do a U-turn. In Cardiff in April 1938, *bottom right*, Gladwins' truck has plenty of room to park while passengers board Brush-built lowheight car 98 at the Tudor Street/Clare Road junction.

While repairs to the sea wall continue at Maesgwyn, Llandudno ex-Bournemouth car 7 runs on the wrong track, *top left*, and slows to regain its proper track via the crossover. In August 1954 Llandudno car 5, one of five bought from Accrington in 1931, makes the descent of the Bodafon Fields right of way to regain Llandudno streets at Craig-y-Don, *bottom left*. The shelter names the stop as Nant-y-Gamar. At Maesgwyn in August 1955 work on sea defences is well advanced, but the seaward track is covered in sand, *above*, while well-filled car 10 heads for Llandudno, bathers head for the beach, and Henry Priestley records the view from an ex-Bournemouth open top car waiting its turn for the single line.

Henry Priestley took the *top left* view near Kingswood terminus, Bristol, on a wet August day in 1938, "just to show the interlaced track". Car 124 is scarcely altered since it began work in 1900. The cyclist takes good care to keep clear of the tracks on this rain-burnished road. In July 1939 Birmingham bogie car 714 of the 1925 series, *bottom left*, has just come up from Gravelly Hill to Park Road junction and the driver is setting the points to turn towards Witton depot.

The pattern of road surfaces and tracks shows up *above* at Lodge Road terminus, where bow-collector equipped Birmingham car 61 of 1905 stands in July 1939. Poster hoardings and tramcars were often the only spots of bright colour in a soot-laden urban landscape.

Over page

At nearly 20 points on the London tramways, change pits were provided to allow cars to change between centre-slot conduit and overhead current collection. Men like these twin brothers at Mile End Road in June 1939, top, lined up the "ploughs" ready to feed them into cars entering the conduit section, using the two pronged fork. E3 type car 190, one of those supplied by London County Council in 1931 to run the Leyton tramways, heads gingerly forward, still on overhead power, past some track repairs. There was always an overlap of conduit and overhead wiring at these change pits, and cars in the other direction would stop immediately before the change point to raise the trolleypole, then accelerate past. The end of the conduit, diverted across the running rails into the pit, would bring the discarded plough bouncing out on its own, always a fascinating operation to see.

The cool and quiet of a tram depot, and those unforgettable smells of gear oil and freshly dried sand. In May 1937 Henry Priestley uses the bulkhead of Coventry car 35 to record open top car 34 in Priestley's Bridge Depot, *left*, but for open top car 31, *above*, he set up his camera on a car step to give a maintenance man's eye view. The wall rising on the right is actually the lower or 'rocker' panel of a tramcar, viewed at close quarters.

Henry Priestley often chose high vantage points, and here at Bristol he excels himself. "I wanted to get that trolley standard," he says, and in April 1939 he records 1895-built car 125's top deck, and beyond it, approaching the Bedminster Parade loop, *top left*, is car 7 of 1900. "I wanted a picture of someone boarding. And that lovely centre pole carrying four wires." And he succeeds, this time in April 1938, with a young lady boarding a car at Old Market, *bottom left*, with trolleypoles disclosing two more cars in front and car 166 about to leave for Nags Head Hill Top. Open tops did not disappear with Bristol trams in 1941, and a boy watches quizzically as Henry Priestley stands to take a picture on Llandudno ex-Bournemouth car 13 at Colwyn Bay terminus, *above*, in August 1953. One of these cars is preserved, restored to its Bournemouth colours. But for twenty years they were synonymous with Llandudno and Colwyn Bay, and part of the elegance went with them.

A London E1 car emerges from Church Crescent, Hackney, *top left*, flanked by new, heavier poles planted for trolleybus wiring. On the Lauriston Road corner, the shop, shut on this Sunday in June 1939, carries advertising for six different brands of cigarettes. Cardiff car 70, reversing at Clarence Road terminus in September 1937, *centre left*, stands alongside a poster announcing Paul Robeson and Cedric Hardwicke in King Solomon's Mines. Not forgetting Idris at the organ. A close look at the *bottom left* picture in Leicester, taken outside the Great Northern station, shows that a flock of sheep is holding up car 92 and other home-going Wednesday rush hour traffic in May 1938. In Birmingham, *above*, bogie car 723 negotiates part of the complex layout of one way street workings in the Cannon Hill area at the Court Road/Edward Road junction in April 1938. Betts, gents outfitter, offers Swallow raincoats at 30s (£1.50).

Brighton, more than just London-by-the-Sea. Until 1939 its open top tramcars, many newly-built, ran on a cluster of 3ft 6in gauge routes radiating from the Aquarium. In August 1934 locally-built car 26 pauses on Queen's Road, *above*, in front of a splendid church built of flints, while Durtnall's removal truck pauses to make a delivery. In April 1939, *top right*, Birmingham 1906-built car 93 passes a Stop-me-and-buy-one uniformed ice-cream man with his tricycle outside the Grove cinema. A year earlier, Cardiff car 14 picks up passengers in Cathedral Road, *bottom right*, as evening shadows lengthen.

In London, *above*, Henry Priestley climbs to the balcony of a block of flats to record E1 class car 558 of 1930 in Tooley Street at Tower Bridge Road, in August 1949. The car has two trolley bases but only one pole; fortunately route 70, like much of inner London's tramway network, is entirely on the centre slot conduit system. Bristol ran 1895-style open top cars from start to finish; car 26, a Milnes product of 1900, swings past Bedminster depot into West Street in April 1939, *top right*. Birmingham 88 of 1906 passes Victoria Park, Smethwick in the same month, *bottom right*; children in these pictures will be in their sixties now.

Merthyr Tydfil had three single-and-loops tram routes totalling 3 ¹/₂ miles, and a fleet of 14 trams, 13 of them second hand. Car 14, *top left*, at Dowlais in April 1938, was bought in 1929 from Birmingham & Midland Tramways. The destination, following B&MT practice, is displayed on the front bulkhead. In July 1938 London E1 car 601, last of the 1930 delivery, loads in Goswell Road at the Aldersgate terminus, *bottom left*, flanked by butchers' delivery cycles and a milkman's hand-propelled 'pram'. And in December 1938 a Bristol motorman, well wrapped in greatcoat and gloves, waits at Colston Avenue while passengers disembark, *above*. Did the ladies with fur wraps travel upstairs? Locally-made signs direct to Bath and Gloucester, but a modern car park sign has appeared, left.

Henry Priestley had seen this Coventry car with an extended destination display and caught it from the top of another, waiting for 51 to clear single track in Stoney Stanton Road, *above*, in May 1937. Coventry car 69 passes the tramway siding into Bell Green station yard, used for delivery of tramway materials, *top right*, in August 1939. Cardiff 23, rebuilt in 1920 from a 1902 model, enters single track in Cowbridge Road, *centre right*. White bands on poles and blackout masks on headlamp and street lights denote wartime; the picture was taken in August 1940. Birmingham car 107 passes the entrance to Tividale depot and works, former Birmingham & Midland headquarters, *bottom right*, in April 1939. Tracks and wires still lead in to the works for power supply purposes.

Stepping out into the road to board a tram in Reading in July 1938, *top left*, near Wokingham Road junction. Overhead fittings for trolleybuses are already visible and the linesmen's tower wagon is parked on the left. Reading's trams ran on 4 ft gauge tracks and this 1903 car was rebuilt in the 1920s. In the same month Henry Priestley photographed London E1 car 907 at Forest Rise at Whipps Cross, *bottom left*. Tracks to the left lead to reserved track along Whipps Cross Road. *Above*, Birmingham balcony car 341 waits for passengers at Selly Oak on a wet day in September 1937. Tramwaymen stand around the Bundy time recorder clock and over the road the church advertises its harvest thanksgiving services.

Previous pages
Moving to the east side of the ex-Rhymney Railway bridge (see earlier page) Henry Priestley records Cardiff car 60, one of the final 1924-25 batch of low height cars, heading towards the city centre along Newport Road a few weeks before the outbreak of the 1939-45 war. Would anyone today push a child in a pushchair across a main road at so acute an angle as the young lady on the left?

Birmingham was at the centre of a vast network of 3ft 6in gauge tram tracks, stretching out into the Black Country towns. *Above*, Birmingham car 808, dating from 1928-9, moves up to the Navigation Street loading point during the last weeks before the Bristol Road routes closed in July 1952. Also on 3ft 6in gauge was the Llandudno & Colwyn Bay Electric Railway; mainstay of its fleet in later years were ten elegant open top cars, secondhand from Bournemouth in 1936. Car 13, 1921-built, *top right*, heads along Penrhyn Avenue in August 1954, while sister car 12 is seen from another open top on Mostyn Street corner, Llandudno, *bottom right*, surrounded by taxis, visitors' cars, and the local council's sightseeing bus fleet.

Over page

As well as being the work of a noted tramway photographer, these pictures have benefitted from the specialised photographic processing facilities of the National Tramway Museum. Photographic archivist Glynn Wilton had to give a series of seven different exposures to bring out the various details of this view of Bath Electric Tramways, taken in September 1937, and many other pictures in this book have required similar care in printing. So, with clarity we see every part of the scene as two of the elegant single deck cars pass on Bath Old Bridge; in the distance an open top car turns towards the Great Western Railway station and the pinnacles of Bath Abbey show above the rooftops. All these cars date from 1904, were built by Milnes, and wore a distinctive livery of bright blue and primrose yellow. A bamboo pole with a hooked end is carried on the side of car 51 for use in dewirements or turning the trolleypole at intermediate terminal points; automatic reversers were provided at most termini and the open top cars had ropes. Buses took over in 1939.

Cyclists show the speed of the photographer's exposure as they blur across the tram tracks. In Coventry, *top left*, car 61 has just negotiated a short piece of interlaced track in Bishop Street in August 1939. Two Birmingham bogie cars pause at the Grove Lane junction with Soho Road, *bottom left*, in March 1939, with notices in their front windows of impending conversion of all the Hockley Depot-based routes to buses on 1 April. Seconds later, a fast-moving car from Dudley or Wednesbury would have filled the lens. At Washwood Heath Depot stop, *above*, bow-collector-equipped car 810 takes up passengers while a builder's Fordson truck demonstrates overtaking a tram on the offside.

Conversion of north London tram routes to trolleybuses was in full swing in July 1938 when Henry Priestley recorded E1 car 1193, one of the 1908-09 batch, *top left*, at Woodford Napier Arms terminus on the edge of Epping Forest. On the poster hoardings, Clark Gable and Myrna Loy in Manhattan Melodrama, and 84,000 new members joined the London Co-op in 1937. In Bristol, *bottom left*, posters for Kodak film as well as the cinema form a background at Nags Head Hill Top in April 1939 to car 124, little changed since it left Milnes' works in 1900. Advertisements swathe the buildings at the corner of Pentonville road, Kings Cross, *above*, as London car 536 emerges from Grays Inn Road one Sunday in June 1938; this is not an E1 but the earlier E type, dating from 1906.

Plymouth staff called the 1924 batch of tramcars "square faces"; the angular English Electric lines of car 133, *above*, show in this 1938 view at the Guildhall. Conduit track but no overhead wires at Tooting Broadway, London, *top right*, in March 1950, where the conductor of ex-Walthamstow 1927-built car 2045 watches the pointsman on the pavement pull the lever to bring the car round the curve. Compare it with the smooth asphalt road and neat overhead wiring at Selly Oak, Birmingham, *bottom right*, where in September 1937 Rednal-bound balcony car 358 waits for car 396 to clear the crossover. Today much has changed at this scene, but the University tower remains in the background.

Over page
Birmingham had already abandoned several tram routes when it opened this section of reserved sleeper track along Sutton New Road in September 1938 to by-pass the narrow Erdington High Street. In May 1953, only a few weeks before the final closure of Birmingham tramways, pedestrians cross with confidence in front of car 563, and already the white stripes of a zebra crossing and an international pattern of no-entry sign point the way into future years. The striped end-blind of the shop, and its end wall, tar-painted for weather protection, are features of the period. And there is not a single television aerial in sight.

Traffic and tramline: A limousine overtakes Reading car 24 on the offside while the tanker lorry, restricted to 20 mph, hangs back on the nearside at Sussex Place loop, Wokingham Road, *top left*. It is July 1938; trolleybus fittings have already been added to the spanwires. In London, *bottom left*, E1 car 949, running on trolley, is about to cross the Mile End Road conduit tracks to reach Burdett Road in June 1939. Another London picture, *top right*, this time with orthochromatic film, shows well turned-out HR2 car 1860 of 1930 in Lewisham Road at John Penn Street. Cyclists overtaking the parked Dennis Pax truck will need to avoid the tram tracks.

Previous pages
Shirley Temple tops the bill at the cinema and trolleybus wiring clings like ivy to the tram wires at Greengate, West Ham, as London Transport E1 car 1296, new in 1910, pauses on its way from Barking to Aldgate in 1938. Boards on the side of the tramcar advertise cheap mid-day fares as well as giving route details.

Leicester 59 pauses at the end of Groby Road in June 1937, *top left*, before turning left on to the Abbey Park Road reserved track and so to the depot. A fine display of deck chairs at the corner shop. Car 169 loads passengers outside Leicester Midland station in May 1938, *bottom left*. A bamboo pole for turning the trolley is hung along the bottom of the car side. With camera held low, giving a child's viewpoint, Henry Priestley captures a crowd of workers boarding city-bound Birmingham car 148 outside West Smethwick Depot, *above*. This B&MT depot was used by Birmingham from 1928 till the last trams ran to Dudley in 1939.

Scrapyard scenes at St Denys, Southampton, *top and bottom left*, in June 1949 when the remaining trams there still had six months to run. The low-built open top cars, with their back-to-back 'knifeboard' seats on top, were designed to fit under the medieval Bargate arch, later by-passed. The balcony cars worked on other routes. One of the open top cars, no. 45 is preserved at the National Tramway Museum and others are being restored locally. Bristol Tramways created their own scrapyard by knocking a hole through the back wall of Kingswood depot and laying tracks into a field, *above*. Car 57 of 1900 is one of about 20 cars Henry Priestley found there in August 1939, following closure of the Zetland road routes in July. Piles of tramcar seats lie to right and left of the picture.

In June 1949, London is still busy healing the scars of wartime bombing, with temporary single storey shops in many places. Trams have been overhauled and their new red and cream paintwork is a bright spot in street scenes of austerity; any new buses available are needed urgently to replace worn-out pre-war buses. London Transport car 552 dates from 1930, one of the final batch of E1 class cars built with bogies and equipment from single deck cars which worked the Kingsway Subway routes till it was deepened to take double decks in 1930-31. Growth of road traffic is such that Henry Priestley would today find it difficult to take up this position for more than a few seconds in the middle of Waterloo Road, looking towards St George's Circus. The Old Vic theatre is still there on the left, and trams seem set to reappear in Croydon, once part of the great London network.